Coffee With Sw[...]
For M[...]

By
RWB

Coffee With Sweet Cream
For Me

Copyright by Robert Brubaker © 2024

All Rights Reserved.

No portion of this book may be reproduced in whole or in part, by any means, except for passages excerpted for purposes of review, without the written permission of the author.

Table of Contents

Introduction v

1860 1

Self-Assessment 2

Fight 3

To Be a Man 4

Vulnerability 5

Fire 6

Living a Circus 7

Books 8

Run 9

Family 10

Candle 11

Time Change 12

Fishing 13

Grace 14

Self Love 15

Cross Creek 16

Ice Cream Truck 17

Bald Eagle 18

Control 19

Angels 20

Cup 21

Sandwich 22

Fences 23

To Save a Penny (For Jen) 24

Shadow... 25

Shame.. 26

Trigger 27

Hungover 28

Alcohol-Free 29

Build Your Better Boat 30

Ocean 31

Anger 32

Pink Cloud 33

Storm.. 34

Winning 35

Looks 36

Cloud Surf.. 38

Scars... 39

Questions 40

Release The Mind 41

Our Bug (for Kyle) 42

Fears... 43

Desire... 44

Bite Your Tongue 45

Lake of a Mirror... 46

Broken Mirror 47

To You For Me 48

My Cross.. 49

Yet.. 50

Chameleon 51

iii

When 52

Broken Bone (for Ryan) 53

Stepping Stone 54

Don't Forget Your Change 55

Intuition 56

Let Others Say and Do 57

Coffee 58

Scared 59

RWB 60

The End 61

Acknowledgments 62

About The Author 64

Introduction

I have tried to make changes in my life over a million times. This results in the same ending of some change but then back to the old ways. I could not pinpoint the flaw in the roller coaster we call life and find the ultimate goal of living happily and proud. I found myself doing everything for others. I had an obligation to please others and also compare myself to others. In doing so, I had zero mindfulness and self-awareness. This is a dangerous recipe to judge oneself and not feel at peace. I wanted to lose weight but would find myself looking to others to see what they had done to do so. I wanted to enrich my mind through reading and writing but would talk myself out of it because others were better than me. I knew living an Alcohol-Free life would bring joy and health, but I was worried that others would label me as having a problem. When speaking, I would draft my thoughts to what I thought others would want to hear instead of saying what I wanted. I began to feel trapped, trapped by society's expectations, the success of friends, and social media's perfection. I was not living my life for me but more to please. I uncovered this through writing poetry.

Poetry is healing, feeling, discovering, and beautiful. There is no right or wrong way to do it. It is about the feeling and self-discovery it gives you when you write or read it. When difficult conversations would arise in my head, I started to say to myself, "For me." A reminder that the only person who can control my feelings is me. I cannot control what they may say. I cannot control if somebody else dislikes my writing. I cannot control if friends think I should do this or that. What I can control is my feelings and reactions to all of the above. Because what I do, or what I say, or what I write is for me.

The collections of my poetry you are about to read were all written during this self-discovery. There is no rhyme or reason (except in the poetry :), just my feelings, written in words. They were written to express what I was feeling at that time. While our lives are stories, they are not linear, and neither is my poetry. It expresses the ups and downs I faced everyday and what I needed to write to understand that particular day. You will find some pictures that accompany some of the poems. These are pictures I took or were taken of me that inspired me to write that poem. Although the poetry was written for me, I hope you can find inspiration and deep meaning to self. My only ask is that you read this for you and share with others as well. If one line in one poem helps one person, all the hours, sweat, and tears put into this are worth it.

I hope you enjoy it. Thank you for reading.

"To you, I dream you know there is no surface."

Much love,

RWB.

1860

I walk into an old building but a new bookstore is in show

I instantly feel the history sweep in my body as this is my story, I know

The outside is made of stone, and the inside is built of wood

If I could, I would have stood there forever

Just smelling and feeling all that would be there before

The story is told that it was built to house whiskey barrels but now is home to a thousand books

You can smell a hint of sweet caramel absorbed in the walls mixed with pen and paper, all nestled in nooks

This building of beauty used to fill booze to those in need, and now it enriches the minds of those who read

It is a symbol of change that has outlasted the test of time

So similar to me this journey of mine

The sign outside of the building of the new bookstore that inspired me.

Rob Brubaker

Self-Assessment

Before I look deep, I have to dig deep

Uncovering things that are difficult can make me weep

Who am I? What am I about? Why do I do what I do?

Just relax; take a breath; it's all about finding you

Hands swell; heart races; I get anxious; why do I make these faces?

Slow down, time will tell, and it's all about finding you

Trauma irks my soul and hits me like thunder

All to leave the imagination to wonder

Do the work, get grounded, meditate to find peace

Before I know it myself, I will get that release

Fight

My mind races like it is on a stage of a big fight

Everyday, every hour, it is in my sight

Whatcha looking at? You don't know me

Wait around, keep looking, and you shall see

It should be simple, easy as can be, but that ain't me

Take a shot, give a shot, and feel KNOW pain

Sweat hydrates and blood glistens; both create stains

Hoping one day someone understands and just listens

Rob Brubaker

To Be a Man

As a man, I am told not to cry

So when the pain hits, my tears run dry

I provide and protect

Honesty to others and to self, respect

I am a man, I yell so proud

Even though at times, saying that is not allowed

I stand as a father, son, and brother, strong

I make mistakes and find myself in the wrong

Go above the clouds and look down from afar

Because being the best man I can be is my north star

Vulnerability

It is a trade

I use my tools

Or it will fade

Remove the noise and hear the sound

When I open the sun

The true me will be round

Rob Brubaker

Fire

To have a flame

I need a fire

To start a fire

I need a flint

To light a flint

I need a fire

My fire, I admire

Living a Circus

Somedays, the pen cannot find the paper

Like the sun cannot find the earth

My energy; my light; my purpose tends to taper

So much going on and I feel like the ringmaster of a circus

Take a step back because today is designed to live

Dig into the soil and rise through the clouds

Look to give and remember, frustration is allowed

Rob Brubaker

Books

Books are the lifeline to feed my mind

Such a powerful tool to help me unwind

Words jump off the pages and meaning joins my blood

My ethos awakens; motive hits my taste bud.

Run

Run away from fears and into my dreams

Live to dream instead of dreaming to live

The intent is to find the crop of my cream

Find my why… don't let my passions die

My resistance is to be and live free

Run, run, run… give it a try

Rob Brubaker

Family

I need family to plant my seed

To have it grow, light I feed

Pull the weeds, and rise will show

It will fight, so hold it tight

Stay together like the strength of a feather

Weather the storms with all my might

My family tree shall never fall

Only stand so ever tall

Coffee With Sweet Cream For Me

Candle

The essence of a candle is a beautiful thing

When I look close, I can hear it sing

The movement is still, but yet so aggressive

It represents life to be ever successive

Light it and let it burn

Before I know it, it will be my turn

This candle represents where I am from. The great state of Ohio. I also bought it in Hilton Head Island, South Carolina which is a favorite vacation spot of mine.

Rob Brubaker

Time Change

Don't let an hour ruin my day

It's my least favorite day, is what I say

Every day is an opportunity to dream

It's only an hour I lost to lay

Slay the day in every way

It's up to me, my mind to scheme

Another day, I get to live; I go yell and scream

Coffee With Sweet Cream For Me

Fishing

Fishing is like wishing

Wishing, in something, I do not have

To have a wish, I have faith

To have faith, I must create

To create, I must throw a line

And when I do, a fish I will find

A picture of me catching a fine-tooth shark off the coast of Hilton Head Island, South Carolina. Doing something, I love in a place I call my second home.

Rob Brubaker

Grace

Embrace the grace

Tough times, I am sure to face

More good than bad

But I live in a world of hate

Live with positivity; no reason to wait

Off my shoulders with the weight

Grace will flow at an amazing rate

Coffee With Sweet Cream For Me

Self Love

When times are tough and rough

I tell myself as I would to others

I will feel euphorically chuffed

Compared to others, I will dig my own grave

I use my shovel to defend the waves

I write and read to feed my needs

Only my hand will fit the glove

For there is only myself to love

Rob Brubaker

Cross Creek

Look across to the other side

Water, rocks, and snakes to get there

The journey is resistant, but what a ride

Doubt and shame are merely a scare

Once I cross, I will feel forever pride

Don't look back, don't you dare

For I have made it across the creek

Me, my mind… strong, no longer weak

This is the Little Miami River in Loveland, Ohio. I frequent this river for mindfulness and to find ideas for my writing.

Coffee With Sweet Cream For Me

Ice Cream Truck

I missed the ice cream truck

It feels as if I have no luck

'Tis tough to show my frustration

I take it out on those who keep me in motion

A little thing to get upset about

A small fish in a big ocean

Important to me as it affects how I feel

Time to take the ice cream and the wrapper, I peel

Rob Brubaker

Bald Eagle

A bald eagle is not bald

But has amazing eyesight

To my sight, it looks extremely strong

But they are mostly feathers bound tight

Their population is in decline; I fear one day, they could be gone

But their fight to exist shows at every campsite

They represent America, the USA

O'er the land of the free and home of the brave, I sing every day

Coffee With Sweet Cream For Me

Control

I can't control the eye of the storm

Or the storms around the world

Society markets me to conform

They are streets ahead

It's what I am told

To unfold

I must be conscious

To have control

It all lies in my subconscious

Rob Brubaker

Angels

Angels befall before they cease

With disruption at ease

When guidance accepted

God and humanity get intercepted

They govern, escort, and protect

Use soft sounds to connect

Have beauty beneath

Above, the sheath

Coffee With Sweet Cream For Me

Cup

Is the cup half empty or half full?

Does it matter?

The matter is to flatter

The substance and smell

Is where I dwell

The amount is only important to sell

But the taste is where I excel

Rob Brubaker

Sandwich

In between dreams and reality lies something I call life

Searching for the deli with no direction

I can barely hear the bread cut by the knife

To ponder what could be above or below

Squeezed like the mustard, ever so slow

Cut the ends off the tomato, and juices will flow

The onion makes me cry to a place when I fly

The sandwich is one with no signs of grease

Lettuce understand, my meal is complete

And time to eat easy, with my peace.

Fences

My fence is my boundary

On the outside, I explore; inside, it protects

It projects my past, good and bad

I give it a pass, as it cannot move

To prove I have changed, it needs a gate

A gate to reflect but to stay in the present

I see a pheasant that sits on my fence

Hence, my sense of creativity it represents

With that comes positivity, I feel

I reel in emotions and think before speak

To have a fence is not to be weak

It helps me seek the barriers I deal with

Rob Brubaker

To Save a Penny (For Jen)

You deserve the happiness to be

To see the stars shine bright like Guy and Bugs' smile

You deserve to love hopelessly and sing with glee

To relax by the ocean and take that free trial

You deserve to run with no finish line

And to take a drive but nowhere to go

You deserve to spend every dime

In that new outfit, go out and show

You deserve to watch your boys grow as they witness

And spend time on you, your body, mind, fitness

You deserve to watch soccer with a blanket and not freeze

And not feel to others as you must please

You deserve to be selfish

And read that book you have been trying to relish

You deserve the happiness to be

Because your life is yours, be ever free

I love you, me, and us

Together we trust

Coffee With Sweet Cream For Me

Shadow

When my body comes between rays of light, my shadow appears

With it comes sadness, gloom, worry, fear

To understand myself, I continue to ponder

But the shadow will not leave even when I wonder

Time to take the Bible off the shelf

The shadow is God's protection of oneself

I am not unescorted or even alone

Then what does this mean? This darkness of clones

It is not evil like folklore says

It allows me to survey inventory every single day

I can question and reflect if I may

But I lead my shadow, not the other way

Rob Brubaker

Shame

Shame is a game I shall not play

There is no winner or loser and it always ends in a tie

As I knot my tie and tie my stomach in knots

I seek the trauma where it arises

But to dig to the root, I avoid my disguises

I have buried my past and the hurt it awaits

But I serve my soul and deliver it on plates

In doing so, I uncover the truth

I nurture it with soil; the fruit will grow

To have no shame, I ease the pain

And then my life will surely flow

Coffee With Sweet Cream For Me

Trigger

A trigger, figuratively speaking, is a knockout punch I did not know was coming

So, I reach for my beverage to let the numbing begin

I begin to let the feelings dissipate, the feelings I am not aware of

I am aware the release has come, but not really sure where they came from

I ask myself in confusion, why is this masking making such a beautiful elusion?

For it only lasts so long before the song comes to end

To defend I say it is how I deal, and makes me feel surreal

But the real reason is I am not dealing with the feelings that arose from my trigger.

Rob Brubaker

Hungover

It is 2:30 am and I wake in a sweat

Why is my pillow soaking wet?

My head is pounding like someone hits me with a hammer

How could this be? It was just yesterday I had such glamor

I reach for my phone to see what I text

If I said the wrong thing to the right person, it could cause such a wreck

Am I having a heart attack? My heart is pounding

Calm down; it is just your anxiety that is hounding

But whom did I see, and what did I say?

I probably pushed many away

Today is a wash; I will stay in bed

And let these thoughts linger in my head

You have done this a million times

Keep going, Bru; you will end up dead

I can't live like this; this is no way to live

It's time to stop for the thousandth time

One more time to flee, to live Alcohol-Free

Coffee With Sweet Cream For Me

Alcohol-Free

I say it is such a magical thing

But it keeps my courage from sing

I say I use it to gather

But when mixed with hurt, it lathers

I say I use it to celebrate

But the torture it brings, I hate

I say I use it to mourn

But in mourning, I feel nothing but torn

I say it makes me more outgoing

But all it does is keep me from growing

I say it numbs the pain

But all it does is make the pain stain

I say I want the world to see

Let's try it to go alcohol-free

Rob Brubaker

Build Your Better Boat

The front of the boat is called the bow

It guides me; sometimes, I don't know how

The back of the boat is called the stern

While serious in direction, It signifies the past, and moving forward, I yearn

The left side of the boat is called the port side

It is marked by red and protects my passengers who accompany my ride

The right side is called the starboard

It protects me, the captain

Where it is easy to see, it is frequently ignored

My boat is called my vessel

I am building my better boat; in it, I nestle

Coffee With Sweet Cream For Me

Ocean

In the ocean, I swim to be

With no land to sea, how can I be forever free?

The breeze hits my head, a reminder of strength

My strokes are gentle, small in length

Sharks all around me; I am in danger

I have nothing to feel but pure anger

The ocean in Riviera Maya, Mexico. Notice the danger flag and my beverage in the sand. How ironic?

Rob Brubaker

Anger

To show anger, I am hostile

To be hostile, I must oppose

To oppose is to disapprove

To disapprove, I must express

To express is to convey a feeling

Feelings come from my reactions

How I react is my actions

Pink Cloud

The pink cloud is the most beautiful vision

Ripples from pink to gray almost look like waves

The sun barely cuts through like a precise incision

A euphoric feeling appears, like being in a new world

Not in a creek, not in an ocean, a place only God can create

This is normal, I am told, to unfold after going alcohol-free

The high I get is better than booze

I will not leave this place; I refuse

Could this be? My life from here on out

The cloud begins to dissipate, a storm I scout

This beautiful sky caught my eye. As soon as I took the picture it went away.

Rob Brubaker

Storm

Thunder and lightning, rain and strain

Wind gusts so hard, all I have to do is to put up my guard

My boat has no shelter; am I in Helter Skelter?

Only time will tell how long this will last

I would have given up in the past

My gut tells me to fight as I recall

Wait around, keep looking, and you shall see

If I do, I will feel KNOW pain

I have to weather this storm from within

And when I do, I will feel this win

A midnight storm that I caught. Before it hit you can see the moon peeping through the clouds. Beautiful picture.

Winning

Winning isn't everything, despite what they say

I have learned more from losing; I confess

Nobody but me can define my success

I do what makes me happy and get others out of my ear

They are just yappy, and what comes next, they fear

Rob Brubaker

Looks

Looks like I won the battle, yet my blood runs deep in my wounds

Looks like the volcano erupted, yet I am covered in lava

Looks like my nest is complete, yet my young are off to build their own better boat

Looks like I can see the finish line, yet I am still so far

Looks like I have lost weight, yet I am carrying it on my shoulders

Looks like I quit drinking yet still feel hungover

Looks like I am enjoying my coffee yet forgot the sugar

Looks like I found myself yet got lost along the way

If I can find pride in my wounds and accept the lava

Guide my young, never finish, and enjoy the stay

Find my sugar and add to my cream

Then you, my friend, are living the dream

Coffee With Sweet Cream For Me

Here is a before and after picture of me. The photo on the top was from June 2023. The photo at the bottom is from March 2024. Change does happen from the inside out.

Rob Brubaker

Cloud Surf

Look up in the sky with an eagle eye

The sun will not fry, a picturesque cloud will say "hi."

The cloud will appear as waves to surf

Like obstacles ahead, I need to swerve

Leg and core strength feeds my heart

And fills my discovery that is about to start

I move with balance between water and air

Knowing that life is not fair

Being in the clouds doing what I love

Anxious thoughts will get rid of

I saw this cloud driving home and thought it looked like an ocean wave.

Coffee With Sweet Cream For Me

Scars

Scars appear when trauma is healed

No more blood; the tissues are sealed

They do not go away, nor does my past

My skin gets replaced very fast

In my mind, it is not the same.

Will I ever get over my shame?

To understand is the first step

Do I recognize that feeling from my youth? Yep

The process has started; it will never end

For scars are what makes me special, and no need to pretend

Rob Brubaker

Questions

What is your greatest gift?

To explore our world at drift

What do you love the most?

To know my family is eternally close

What is your biggest fear?

That time will run out while my purpose is near

What is your biggest dream?

To inspire others with a gleam

What lesson is important to you?

Forgive, and you will be forgiven, too

What lesson shall you give?

With your life, live

Release The Mind

What should I do? Where do I need to be?

Who needs me right now?

Squirrels?

How do I focus on one?

They are everywhere.

When is it due? Past the deadline. How?

I breathe with such heavy air

What to do to release the mind?

I need something quick and easy

A drink I quickly find

I find quickly it does the trick; the next day feels queasy

This is not the solution to the problem I have

The answer is there for me to find

I may need to subtract to add

To get the equation of releasing the mind

Rob Brubaker

Our Bug (for Kyle)

Our bug is small but filled with energy

Energy of laughter and love

It is the star of its own documentary

It knows what it wants and gets what it needs

There is only one bug like the one we were given

In the roots is where it feeds

We have never seen one so driven

A bug annoys us at the ready

But for some reason, our bug keeps us steady

Coffee With Sweet Cream For Me

Fears

I cannot hide from them or face them head-on

If I do, they will last forever long

Attack it like running into a storm

Don't do what everybody else does and conform

Understand that perfection is a myth

And me and my fears, I will stand with

Rob Brubaker

Desire

To desire does not inspire

Everybody has the wire to desire

To want and wish is easy to see

It is hard to truly find me

Coffee With Sweet Cream For Me

Bite Your Tongue

They say if I don't have anything nice to say

Then don't say anything at all

I have broken this rule in every way

Like biting my tongue, restraint hurts

It eats away at me like a wolf does to a deer

Dissolving any feeling of having guts

If I don't have anything nice to say

Then I say it but in a respectful way

Rob Brubaker

Lake of a Mirror

I find a lake that looks like a mirror

So much trauma in this water

One of my rocks has sunk to the bottom

A smaller image of me

Only God can make matter float

And now that rock sits with ease

Looking into the lake with me

Norris Lake in Tennessee. This lake has many fond memories spent with friends and has a strong tie to this poem.

Coffee With Sweet Cream For Me

Broken Mirror

A broken mirror is shattered and in a million pieces

Sometimes, I know how it broke, and other times I do not

It looks complete, but with so many disconnects

Its fight to stay together is everything it seizes

When it breaks, I remove it from its permanent spot

I move it to a place where only dust can collect

In the cold, I cannot look at it as it freezes

But when it thaws, I can, and my blood gets hot

The image that appears is my intellect

Rob Brubaker

To You For Me

To you, I want to energize

For me, it helps galvanize

To you, I want to inspire

For me, it recognizes my misfires

To you, I give hope

For me, it eliminates mope

To you, I want you to feel

For me, it helps me heal

To you, know that you can

For me, it makes me a better man

To you, I encourage you to share

For me, it brings out care

To you, I crave you to express

For me, it soothes my distress

To you, I want you to love yourself

For me, it taught me to love myself

To you, I dream you know there is no surface

For me, well, I now have a purpose

Coffee With Sweet Cream For Me

My Cross

I wear it around my neck

In my shirt and by my heart

It's made of nails

And I am tough like them

It signifies my faith

On the back, it has a date

For He will always be with me

The cross that I wear around my neck.

Rob Brubaker

Yet

Life is a journey yet beautiful

I get sick yet I recover

People die yet children are born

I lose faith yet find God

I fear storms yet admire them

I get burned by the sun yet can't survive without it

I get upset when grass dies yet grows back again

Flowers die in off-season yet I buy new ones in season

I lose my hearing yet the wisdom I hear

I lose my eyesight yet find purpose in my sight

I get in fights yet find more love

I am hurt by others yet learn to forgive

I care for my young yet know they will care for me one day

Chameleon

A chameleon is the wizard of all lizards

Because they can change the color of the one given by their mother

They can turn pink, blue, green, red, or purple at the wink of the eye

I see it on the outside, but the change happens on the inside

Let's say they wear their weather on their leather

When it is sick or stressed, it uses black and white to express

But when filled with joy, it is using its ploy

When excited, it turns bright to show fright

While it shows a range of colors, it never changes with anger

Maybe it is not a wizard and more like me

My colors of change I must trust.

Rob Brubaker

When

I don't feel cold when I have seen the sun

It's not hard to swim when I have been on the island

The music isn't loud when I feel the beat

It is never cloudy when I see them as art

The moon is not spooky when I know it is light

There is no past when I am living in the moment

The internet never goes down when I connect with others

I am not old when I feel young

There is no harm when I don't allow it

There is no fall when I get back up

I can be myself when I love myself

Coffee With Sweet Cream For Me

Broken Bone (for Ryan)

Bones are strong but can be broken

It is your token to build strength

At length, you give it time

You do not whine or feel confined

You pour your courage without a worry

As you deal, I see your sparkle flurry

I am proud of you as you heal

There are no bones in your heart to find

I love your heart with all of mine

Rob Brubaker

Stepping Stone

Steps of stones are a step in the right direction

A connection to get me from one place to the next

Up a hill or through the garden

I make connections along the way

Do not use them; my relationships will stay

I may be timid to take that first step

For fear of falling with one misstep

But if I don't, I will not know

What my show is meant to be

Stones of steps that I use to get up and down to the Little Miami River in Loveland, Ohio.

Coffee With Sweet Cream For Me

Don't Forget Your Change

I have paid for life and received my change

How do I keep that change in my pocket?

This new feeling, at times, 'tis strange

I am living the life I always dreamed of

Free of anxiety, fear, and self-doubt

Without a doubt, this cannot last. Or can it?

My heart is full, but knowingly, challenges ahead will come about

I shout with pride that I have the tools, but only a fool would think I have made it

A sharp knife that becomes dull will no longer cut

A hammer without a nail has no purpose

For all of it to stick, the light needs to continue to flicker

Rob Brubaker

Intuition

I needed a new lawnmower, to the store, I go

They had so many to choose from and all of them on show

My research was complete, and I was set on one

Confidence in buying it should be extremely fun

As I put the box on the cart, the corner cut my hand

I could have seen this as a sign of a wound needing aid to band

I pushed it to the checkout when a stranger came and said. "Tread lightly with that; it is not the best sled to shred some hay."

In the past, I would have let my head get to me

Take his comment, and my cut as ever true to be

I listened to my intuition and went along with my mission in my own way.

My mower is fantastic, regardless of what others seem to say

This is the lawnmower I went for and went home with.

Coffee With Sweet Cream For Me

Let Others Say and Do

Everyone will always have an opinion, as we are living beings who walk the earth like minions

A million times, I have let others say and do

A million times, I have listened to what they knew

I knew this was a challenge of mine to make my change stick

I used to let it get to me like a trick on my mind

In the thick of the moment, I must recognize my feelings

The wheeling and dealing with my head space; where do I go to trace?

I now face this obstacle head-on with all my might

I cannot control it any other way, so I let others say and do

Rob Brubaker

Coffee

Coffee is my new drink of choice

I chose it because freedom comes out loudly in my voice

I prefer caramel flavor mixed with sweet cream

Ironic as it represents the smell I got from 1860 and allows me to dream

Even my coffee is smiling back at me.

Coffee With Sweet Cream For Me

Scared

This is everything I have been scared to say

To share with the world in every way

It is my feelings written in words

For you to read here, it unfolds

I am no longer scared of me

I love myself for all to see

Rob Brubaker

RWB

My pen calls me RWB

The man I always wanted to be

I am not perfect and have a past of mistakes

But I am shedding my skin that comes off in flakes

More mistakes to come but I do so with grace

My purpose is to inspire at God's pace

I ride the waves when they come

And now understand where I came from

I use the waves to surf my life

Raising our children with my beautiful wife

Only God knows what is next for me

That is me, RWB.

Coffee With Sweet Cream For Me

The End

It is time for this book to end

For new chapters, I have to write and projects to attend

The mirror is not cracked, as you have more life to pack

You have only one life to live, so remember to give

Stop and breathe and feel the breeze

Love yourself as you do to others

Understand feelings and know your colors

There is no end when you live for the moment

Go find that missing component

Your book is not over, as you shall see

As this book is to you but for me

The End.

Acknowledgments

This work of poetry would not have been possible if there were not so many special people in my life.

I would like to thank my wife, Jen. When I told you I wanted to write this book, you showed nothing but support. Thank you for continuing to believe in us and our family. You have shown me what true love is. To my Mom and Dad, you never gave up on me, no matter the situation. Your strength in your marriage has shown me how to navigate challenging times and celebrate great ones. You have taught me perseverance, unconditional love, and grace. To my sons, Ryan and Kyle, you amaze me every day and make me proud to be your Dad. Your love and laughter are infectious. Always remember to believe in yourself, don't let others tell you differently, and treat others with respect. To my sisters, you have been trailblazers for me. You protect your younger brother and never say no when I need you. It is an honor to watch your respective families grow. To my nieces and nephews, you make life so much fun for me. Seeing extensions of family continue to grow makes me smile daily. I am excited to see what is in store for you all. To all my inlaws, you are family to me, and I learn something from all of you every day. Thank you for the support and love you provide for me and those closest to me. To my friends, you make me laugh and are there for me when I cry. I am blessed to have so many of you in my life. Ruari, Jen, and your team, your passion for creating new ways of life for so many across the world is inspiring. Your practices and innovation with One Year No Beer have had a drastic impact on mine. To Faolan, Gary, and Olly, you believed in me and have taught me many tools to learn about myself and deal with my feelings. I am ever grateful for being connected to you. To my CCS cohort, you know who you are. All across the world, we found friendship, connection, and hope. You were some of the first to know that I was going to write this book. I am here for you in any way you need.

Coffee With Sweet Cream For Me

I would also like to thank my project manager, Collin. You dealt with all my ideas and changes throughout this journey with nothing but support.

Lastly, to my readers. Without you, this message cannot be shared. Whatever life throws at you, know that you can embrace the grace with it and make the change that you want to. I am rooting for all of you.

-RWB-

About The Author

Society calls him Rob, his friends call him Bru, and his pen calls him RWB. RWB is on a mission to show anybody willing to listen that change is possible. Through research and poetry, he believes that change happens from the inside out. His own discovery of himself on the inside has shown drastic health benefits on the outside. He is an alumnus of Ohio State University and an advocate of the alcohol-free movement. RWB resides in Loveland, Ohio, with his wife and two sons. He can be reached at rwbpoetry@gmail.com for a connection.

Printed in Great Britain
by Amazon